MYSTERIES

OF THE ANCIENT WORLD

THE VIKINGS
SAGA

PETER SCHLEDERMANN

WEIDENFELD & NICOLSON
LONDON

On an August day in 1978 I was excavating an ancient house ruin on a small island on the central east coast of Ellesmere Island in the Canadian High Arctic. The collapsed sod house had been built more than 700 years ago by Thule culture Eskimos, ancestors of all present day Inuit in Canada and Greenland.

I was removing floor debris near a stone-lined meat pit when my trowel struck a hard object. Carefully I brushed away the dirt and lifted the find up to have a closer look. I could hardly believe my eyes – in my hand I held a lump of rusted, interwoven iron rings – a piece of medieval chain mail! Later in the day I was about to reach the bottom of the meat pit when the trowel once again struck iron – a Viking ship rivet in a 13th-century house ruin in the High Arctic!

Stone showing a Viking ship.

Skraeling Island, where the greatest concentration of Norse artefacts were found in ancient winter-house ruins, built by Thule culture Inuit.

Uncovering the Vikings

The discovery of chain mail was as remarkable as the fact that we had decided to investigate the island at all. The name had intrigued us, Skraeling Island, so named by a Norwegian explorer, Otto Sverdrup, who had wintered in the area between 1898 and 1899. We surmised that Sverdrup had seen Eskimo house ruins on the island, since the word *skraeling* was often used in the old Norse sagas with reference to Indians and Eskimos.

During the following field seasons we discovered many more Norse artefacts, including ship rivets, iron wedges, a carpenter's plane, pieces of woven woollen cloth, box sides made from oak, barrel bottoms, single chain-mail rings and

*T*he interior of winter-house ruin 6 on Skraeling Island, where a lump of chain mail and the first Viking ship rivet were discovered.

*C*lose-up of the interwoven iron rings making up the rusted lump of chain mail from house 6.

*O*ne of the many complete Viking ship clinch nails (rivets) from Skraeling Island.

many pieces of iron and copper. In one house we discovered a small piece of carved driftwood showing a distinctly non-Inuit face; perhaps an Inuit carving representing one of the Norsemen who had brought the many objects found in the houses? Radiocarbon dating of some of the Norse items and refuse from the winter houses implied that the dwellings had been used somewhere between AD 1250 and 1300.

The evidence left us with many unanswered questions. Where and when had

the Inuit and the Norsemen first met? Had the Norsemen actually brought their ship into the High Arctic and why? Had the ship been crushed in pack ice and abandoned? Did the Norsemen winter with the Inuit on the little island and later return to their settlements in southern Greenland?

The author uncovering a large piece of woven woollen cloth in one of the Skraeling Island houses. The cloth was later radiocarbon dated to about AD 1200.

Wooden figurine found in a house ruin on Skraeling Island, showing facial features of a distinctly non-Inuit person.

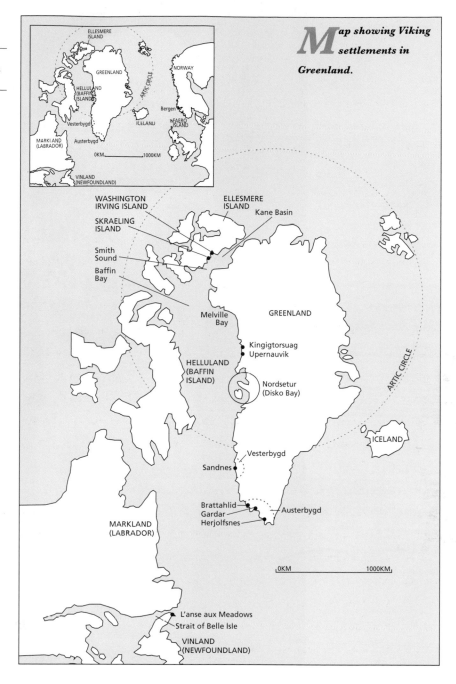

*M*ap showing Viking settlements in Greenland.

Banishment and Discovery

During the many Viking voyages between Norway and Iceland it was inevitable that the mariners occasionally got blown off course by storms in the North Atlantic. On one such occasion the sagas tell of Gunnbjorn who survived a violent gale to find himself approaching a strange, forbidding coast filled with rocky skerries. When he finally reached Iceland his story was told far and wide, eventually reaching the ears of an ill-tempered Norseman named Eirik the Red. On several occasions the quarrelsome Eirik had used his sword to settle disputes, killing a number of his opponents. In the spring of AD 982 he was tried at the local district Thing (parliamentary assembly) and banished from Iceland for three years. Eirik and his friends had little doubt about the outcome of the trial and were well prepared. His ships were loaded with livestock and food, tools and hunting gear, family and field hands, everything he needed to survive in the land he planned to investigate, the land Gunnbjorn had seen.

For three years Eirik the Red explored the south-west coast of this new land. Impressed with what he saw as he sailed along the shores of the immense fiords bordered by cascading streams and rich pastures he named it Greenland. As he sailed deeper and deeper into the fiords, he marvelled at the luxurious summer growth of grass and the size of willow thickets and dwarfed birch trees. Occasionally they came across traces of older habitations and fragments of skin boats, but never a soul came into view – the land he took possession of was empty of people. The abandoned habitations he encountered may have been occupied by Irish hermits, perhaps some of the people the Norsemen had originally enslaved or chased out of Iceland many decades before. The camps may also have been used by Dorset people, the last of the palaeo-eskimos, who occupied much of Greenland for more than 3,000 years. At the time of Eirik the Red's exploration it is very likely that some of these Dorset people still occupied the northerly regions of Greenland.

*A*lthough *popularly held to be an agressive people, who came by sea to raid and loot, modern scholarship has revealed other facets of the Norse character.*

Eirik the Red returned to Iceland, where he spoke in such glowing terms about his discoveries that many chieftains decided to join him on his return to Greenland the following year. In the spring of AD 986 a large fleet of 25 vessels set sail, each vessel brimming with cattle, sheep, pigs, horses, dogs, tools and food. Most of the vessels were overloaded and only 14 completed the voyage. Eirik had already chosen the place he and his family would settle, Brattahlid, an excellent location on the west shore of what became known as Eiriksfiord.

Not long after the first chieftains established themselves in the southernmost Greenlandic settlement they called Austerbygd, Bjarne Herjolfsson got lost on his way to Greenland. After days of drifting in thick fog he spied a low land covered with vast stretches of forest. Eventually Bjarne and his crew found their way back to Austerbygd where they told of their discovery. Eirik the Red's son Leif was the first to explore the land to the west. He sailed along the immense, sandy shores of

Markland (Labrador) and established a settlement at the northernmost promontory of Newfoundland, a place now called L'Anse aux Meadows, within the territory the Norsemen called Vinland. Later explorers to the New World included Leif's brother Thorval, who was killed in battle with Indians. Leif's sister Freydis also sailed to Vinland, a voyage fraught with internal bickering and murder. One of the more impressive Norse explorers was the wealthy merchant Thorfinn Karlsefni who, with a contingent of more than 160 people, spent several years in Vinland. There his wife Gudrid gave birth to Snorre, the first European child born in the New World.

*E*xcavation of the area revealed layers of refuse spanning 350 years of occupation coming to an end about AD 1350, the time Vesterbygd was abandoned.

*B*rattahlid, the site of Eirik the Red's farm and for generations the centre of political power in Norse Greenland.

*T*he spectacular
location of
Herjolfsnes, the first
destination of Norsemen
upon reaching the south
coast of Greenland and
probably one of the last
areas to be occupied by
Norse Greenlanders
around AD 1450.

Norse Greenland

For over 200 years the Norse settlements in Greenland expanded. The original settlement by Eirik the Red had taken place during a turbulent period of Christian conversion of the Nordic lands. Eirik's wife, Thjodhild, embraced the Christian religion and arranged, under some protest from her heathen husband, the construction of a small church at Brattahlid. Over the years the Catholic Church established several monasteries and erected at least 14 churches. In 1126 the first Bishop of Greenland, Arnald, took up residence at the Gardar episcopal seat in Einarsfiord, not far from Brattahlid.

Austerbygd contained the largest number of people and farms. Farther

*E*irik the Red's Brattahlid; the great hall from the north.

*T*ypical Norse farmstead location in Vesterbygd (Western Settlement). The greener vegetation outlines the old irrigated homefield area.

View from the old Norse Sandnes estate in the inner part of the Ameralla Fiord, one of the large fiords that made up the Norse Vesterbygd settlement.

north on the west coast of Greenland was the settlement of Vesterbygd, with 90 farms and four churches. The seat of power in Vesterbygd was the Sandnes estate, owned at one stage by the merchant and Vinland explorer Thorfinn Karlsefni.

The Norse Greenlanders represented the western-most outpost of European culture. They lived as crofters, raising sheep, goats and as many cattle as the irrigated homefields could sustain. Winters were long and cold and feed was often scarce. The trade link with Europe was very important to the Greenlanders, who needed iron, wood for ship building and repairs, grain and a few luxuries like silk and wine afforded only by the wealthier families. In return they could offer only a few valuable items such as walrus hides and tusks, narwhal tusks (thought to have magical properties), homespun woollen cloth and falcons, treasured by royalty and noblemen alike.

In Pursuit of Ivory

The most important hunting ground for walrus and narwhals was far north of Vesterbygd in an area the Norsemen called Nordsetur. Most scholars consider Nordsetur to be the area known as Disko Bay. The Norse hunters travelled north from Vesterbygd

Walrus hides and tusks were two of the most important items used by Norse Greenlanders to barter for European trade goods.

and Austerbygd as soon as the frozen seas allowed passage. As the decades grew into centuries, increasing hunting pressure necessitated exploration farther northward along the rugged Greenlandic coast. The Norsemen faced other difficulties. When Eirik the Red first set foot on Greenlandic soil, the northern hemisphere was experiencing a warmer climate, with diminishing drift ice and easier navigation. A greater extent of open water in the polar seas allowed more driftwood to reach the Arctic shores, providing plenty of building materials for dwellings and ships. The growth of vegetation was enhanced by the milder climate, as was the regeneration of hay-fields on the Greenlandic farms. By the turn of the 13th century conditions had already been deteriorating for some time, slowly at first, then more noticeably; small cottagers and landholders found it difficult to maintain their meagre livestock, and indebtedness to wealthy chieftains and the Church increased.

Norse–Inuit Contact

The 13th century brought dangers of another kind. The Norsemen were no longer the only inhabitants of Greenland. A migration of Inuit tribes that had begun far to the west in Alaska reached the shores of Greenland. The gateway was Smith Sound, a relatively narrow, 45 km wide stretch of water or ice, depending on the season, separating Ellesmere Island and Greenland. While the Norsemen ventured farther northward in pursuit of sea mammals

Remains of one of the two ancient cairns discovered by Captain Nares in 1875.

the Eskimos crossed Smith Sound and began a steady push southward. It was not long before the first meetings took place between the two peoples; Inuit, superbly adapted to an Arctic way of life and Norsemen pursuing a life as farmers and hunters, a life very much rooted in another world.

The Norsemen were familiar with *skraelings*, the natives they encountered on their voyages to Vinland and Markland, where all attempts to establish permanent settlements had been successfully repulsed by the Indians. The Norsemen were easily outnumbered and carried no fighting arms unfamiliar to the Indians, unlike the Spanish who centuries later made such a dramatic and devastating entry into Central America.

The *skraelings* from northern Greenland were different. The Norsemen must have been impressed with the Inuit sea mammal hunting prowess. The Inuit were part of the Thule culture, characterized, among other things, by their ability to hunt bowhead whales from large skin-covered umiaqs in the open sea, and harpoon walrus and narwhals from their sleek kayaks. For the Norsemen there was good reason to offer whatever the Inuit might

*I*vory needle-case from one of the Skraeling Island houses, showing, in style and decoration, that the Inuit occupants originated in Alaska.

*D*rawing of the two cairns discovered by George Nares in 1875. The cairns were most probably constructed by members of a Norse expedition exploring the Kane Basin area in the 13th century.

desire in trade for ivory and walrus skins. The Inuit may have been less interested in trade, although the Norse iron was superior to the iron flakes they obtained from meteorites in north-west Greenland.

A Norse Voyage of Discovery

The encounter with the Inuit may have encouraged the Norsemen to explore for better hunting grounds farther northward. In 1814, a small, flat stone was found near three stone cairns on a small island near Upernavik, just south of Melville Bay. Inscribed on the stone was a runic message telling of three men

*W*ashington *Irving* Island on the edge of *Kane Basin, where Captain George Nares found two ancient cairns in 1875.*

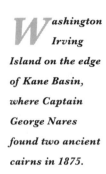

29

who had constructed the nearby cairns and made the runes some-time during early spring, perhaps around AD 1300. The Norse may have travelled hundreds of kilometres north of Upernavik. In early August 1875 the British explorer Sir George Nares had brought his two vessels, *Alert* and *Discovery*, across Smith Sound to Ellesmere Island. About 80 km north of Skraeling Island he stopped in the ice near a prominent island which would provide him with a splen-did view out over the ice-choked Kane Basin and the route north-ward. On top of Washington Irving Island he discovered, much to his surprise, two stone cairns some distance apart. Nares judged the cairns to be quite ancient because of the lichen growth on the stones. Who had constructed the cairns? After searching unsuccess-fully for a message Nares and his men dismantled the cairns and built a new one. Only a few other people visited the island during the next hundred years, including a Royal Canadian Mounted Police constable, whose curiosity about the ancient cairns brought him to the top of the island in 1939.

In 1979, with more than fifty Norse artefacts in hand, we felt that the idea of Norsemen having constructed the two ancient cairns on Washington Irving Island was quite believable. Our first visit was disheartening. Not only did bad weather cut our investigation short, we discovered with great disappoint-ment that Nares's cairn had been destroyed. In 1995 we returned to spend sev-eral days on the island. Just north of the remains of Nares's cairn we located the scattered boulders of what was undoubtedly the remains of one of the two ancient 'Norse' cairns. Our careful search of the surrounding stones and boul-ders did not identify the original builders – disappointing but not surprising.

One scenario may be that a small group of Norse explorers encountered Inuit hunters just south of Melville Bay. Barter led to information about fabulous sea-mammal hunting and large open-water areas to the north. The

*R**emains of the Herjolfsnes church.*** Norsemen chose to cross Melville Bay and continued northward. Seeing the tall, ice-clad mountains of Ellesmere Island only a short sailing distance away, they crossed Smith Sound and continued northward until they reached Washington Irving Island. The ice may have prevented any further progress, or massive floes of pack ice may have crushed their vessel. Two cairns were erected on top of the island followed by an attempt to return south. Inuit hunters encountered the struggling Norsemen and – then what? Did they help them or kill them? Did they invite them to spend the winter on Skraeling Island? Were the many Norse items in the Inuit houses tokens of gratefulness or booty? We shall probably never know.

*R*emains of the
 *Norse Hvalso
church in Austerbygd
(Eastern Settlement).
According to old
documents a
wedding took place
here in AD 1408.*

Demise of the Norse Settlements

If the Norse expedition into the High Arctic was less than successful, so was the continuation of the Norse settlements in southern Greenland. By AD 1350, the bishop's deputy, Ivar Baardsson, from Gardar in Austerbygd, could report that upon visiting the more northerly settlement, Vesterbygd, to investigate rumours of trouble with the Inuit, he had found neither heathens nor Christians in the area, although cattle and sheep had been found roaming the fields. Vesterbygd had been abandoned. If the deputy's report is at all trustworthy, and many believe it is, we are left with more questions than answers. Archaeological investigations tend to confirm that the excavated farms were abandoned about the time of Baardsson's visit. Yet, so far, we have no record of a sudden appearance of Norsemen from Vesterbygd in Iceland or anywhere else. What happened to the people?

We know that climatic conditions had been deteriorating. Worsening ice conditions, particularly in the Austerbygd region which was imprisoned for most of the summer by the *storis*, a broad belt of polar pack ice. Increasing numbers of Inuit migrated southwards, competing successfully with Norse hunters. Similar

A 19th-century drawing of a Viking ship off the west coast of Greenland.

competition for game took place in the autumn, when the Inuit headed inland to hunt caribou in regions used by the Norsemen.

The Inuit and the Norsemen probably engaged in barter, however there are relatively few Inuit items on the Norse farms and small amounts of Norse finds in old Inuit settlements. When the Moravians established a mission in West Greenland in the early 18th century, much was made of collected Inuit stories telling of fierce battles and much violence between the Norsemen and the Inuit; the Inuit burning down farms while the Norsemen attacked Inuit camps killing everyone in sight. Many of these stories are thought to be quite exaggerated. The burdens of life in the Norse colonies were also made heavier in the middle of the 13th century, when King Haakonsson of Norway annexed the former free state of Greenland to his kingdom. A trade monopoly was enforced and taxation was increased. The Norse crofters were squeezed between the Church and the State, both of which expropriated farms – either in lieu of unpaid taxes or as a means of securing the owner an easier passage to Heaven. The trade monopoly resulted in fewer and fewer trade vessels touching the shores of Greenland; Europe's most westerly colony was almost completely isolated.

About the middle of the 14th century calamity

Remains of Norse shepherd's hut overlooking the inner part of Ameralla Fiord.

struck Scandinavia in the form of the deadly plague that periodically ravaged most of Europe. In Norway, the most important trade centre, Bergen, was particularly hard hit. It was from here the so called 'Greenland Knarr' departed on its infrequent trade voyages to Greenland and it may be more than a coincidence that Ivar Baardsson found no people in Vesterbygd just after the time when the plague ravaged Bergen. A late summer arrival in Vesterbygd of one

trading vessel carrying plague-infested rats and fleas would have devastated the small community. No large numbers of skeletons were ever found on the excavated farms or in mass graves.

The tantalizing possibility remains that many of the Vesterbygd people headed westward to reasonably familiar territories in Labrador and the St Lawrence river area. No solid evidence supports this idea, only occasional and always controversial discoveries, such as the Kensington Stone in Minnesota,

the 'Viking' tower on Rhode Island and isolated finds of coins, axes and swords. Some people are convinced that strange stone constructions and longhouse ruins on the Ungava peninsula originated with the Norse. The Vesterbygd abandonment remains a mystery.

The retreat from Vesterbygd did not end the Norse era in Greenland. In Austerbygd the Norsemen continued to work their farms and attended church services, but time was running out. The Inuit moved relentlessly southward, all the way around the southern tip of Greenland and up the east coast. The *storis* jammed the shores all summer long, preventing easy communication between farms in the inner fiord areas. Pirates had become a considerable hazard to traders in the North Atlantic. Small isolated settlements, like those in south Greenland, would have provided an easily obtained bounty of livestock and slaves. At

The east wall of Hvalso church.

some time between AD 1450 and 1500 the last church bell was carefully lowered from its tower and stowed away with all other church valuables in the waiting ship; the farms were abandoned; and the Norsemen left. From their kayaks and umiaqs the Inuit may have watched the last ship sail away from the shores of what was now to be their exclusive domain, a land that had sustained the Norsemen for nearly 500 years.

PHOTOGRAPHIC ACKNOWLEDGEMENTS

Cover Archiv für Kunst und Geschichte London
[AKG]; page 3 Weidenfeld & Nicolson
[WN]/Antik Varisk-topografiska Arkivet;
pp.4–5, 6, 7t, 7b, 8, 9 Peter Schledermann [PS];
p. 12tl WN; p. 12–13 WN/Universitets Old
Saksamling, Oslo; pp. 14, 15, 16;
p. 18 WN/Nationalmuseet/Copenhagen;
pp. 19, 20–21 PS; p. 22 Zefa Pictures;
pp. 24–5, 26l, 26–7, 28–9, 31, 32–3;
p. 34–5 AKG; pp. 36–7, 38–9 PS.

THE
VIKINGS
SAGA

First published in Great Britain 1997
by George Weidenfeld and Nicolson Ltd
The Orion Publishing Group
5 Upper St Martin's Lane
London WC2H 9EA

Text copyright © Peter Schledermann, 1997
The moral right of the author has been asserted
Design and layout copyright © George Weidenfeld
and Nicolson Ltd, 1997

A CIP catalogue record for this book is available
from the British Library
ISBN 0 297 823140

Picture Research: Joanne King

Design: Harry Green

Typeset in Baskerville